PREFACE

This is an expose which walks in the very footsteps of Joshua in the Bible. It is an in-depth magnifier to discover the principles used by Joshua to write his name with gold in this life and the life which is to come. As we learn from the people of old we will better understand the ways of God. The heroes of faith lived in different eras of life and came from diverse backgrounds. In an interesting era of the age of the world today, the foundation which the people of old stood on to stand tall above their enemies still works today and forever. Join me in this microscopic view on aspects of the life of Joshua.

ACKNOWLEDGEMENT

I would like to acknowledge Rev. Panin Darkwa Koampah for several years of mentoring.

DEDICATION

For Mr. James Appiakorang, Dr. Cyril Amankwah, Dr. Bright Prempeh, Mr. David Mensah and Mr. Ransford Okyem, you have been wonderful friends over the years.

Published by OBF Global

ISBN : 978-9988-8867-4-5

TABLE OF CONTENT

CHAPTER FIVE.................CONTENDING FOR THE PROMISE

CHAPTER ONE

THE BAD CIRCUMSTANCE AND YOUR PURPOSE

THE GREAT PROPHET

The life of Moses presents one of the finest subjects for the pen of a Jewish or Christian historian. Moses was one of the great leaders reported from the pen of historians. His institutions breathe a spirit of freedom, purity and intelligence. He was the epitome of justice, love, honor, and obedience to God.

Moses molded the character of the Hebrews and transformed them from a nation of shepherds into a people of fixed residence and agricultural habits. The influence of Moses on Israel has permeated the world with his leadership and governance in raising a people and a nation which still exist in our present world.

Moses was distinguished for his meekness, patience and firmness. There was no other prophet in the land of the Hebrews who could be compared with Moses. No prophet ever arose like Moses, whom the Lord knew face to face. God did not choose to speak to Moses through visions and dreams. The Lord chose to speak to Moses as friends speak to one another.

The Prophet Moses worked great signs and wonders before the sight of the children of Israel. Moses was a man of terror to the enemies of the Israelites. The fear of Moses was upon the Egyptians all the days of his life. There was no leader in Israel who could be compared to Moses in signs and wonders with mighty works in the entire history of Israel.

And there arose not a prophet since in Israel like unto Moses, whom the LORD knew face to face, In all the signs and the

wonders, which the LORD sent him to do in the land of Egypt to Pharaoh, and to all his servants, and to all his land, And in all that mighty hand, and in all the great terror which Moses shewed in the sight of all Israel.

DEUTERONOMY 34:10-12

Among all the succeeding prophets, none was found so eminent or as highly privileged as Moses. With the other prophets, God spoke to them by dreams and visions. With Moses, God spoke face to face with the closest familiarity and greatest friendship. There was truly a great prophet who ever lived among the land of the living; this man was no one else but Moses.

LOSING A GREAT MAN

So Moses the servant of the LORD died there in the land of Moab, according to the word of the LORD. And he buried him in a valley in the land of Moab, over against Beth-peor: but no man knoweth of his sepulchre unto this day. And Moses [was] an hundred and twenty years old when he died: his eye was not dim, nor his natural force abated. And the children of Israel wept for Moses in the plains of Moab thirty days ....

DEUTERONOMY 34:5-8

It was a day of deep sorrow and wailing when Moses died. The children of Israel were now in such a terrible season. The one who had become a symbol of unity for the people of Israel was no more. The whole nation looked up to him for guidance and others sought for mentorship from Moses.

One of the people who Moses mentored was Joshua. Moses had been the teacher and counselor of Joshua for many years. Joshua looked up to Moses for direction in all areas of his life. In the entire life of Joshua, Moses had been both a father figure and a mentor. Moses had been a great counselor in the life of Joshua.

The loss of Moses through his death was a sad experience for the whole of Israel. For somebody like Joshua, it was a very bitter and a peril experience for him. Joshua had lost his father, guide, counselor, and mentor when Moses died. He did lose the father-figure in his walk with God.

LIFE MUST GO ON

Now after the death of Moses the servant of the LORD it came to pass, that the LORD spake unto Joshua the son of Nun, Moses' minister, saying, Moses my servant is dead; now therefore arise, go over this Jordan, thou, and all this people, unto the land which I do give to them, [even] to the children of Israel.

JOSHUA 1:1-2

There are times in our lives it seems the heavens have been shut over our heads and evil has befallen us. This was the same experience Joshua had when Moses died. Joshua was in such a tough situation like he had never experienced before. In such a difficult circumstance, God had a divine plan for that season. Many people do not respond to the call and direction of God in tough times.

Life must still go on after a painful separation. Although it can sometimes become very hard to bear the separation of someone you are used to and so close, life must still move on when they are no more with you. Isaiah, the prophet had to learn this hard fact when king Uzziah died. Uzziah was no doubt one of the great kings the people of Israel ever had.

Uzziah's long reign of about fifty-two years is said to be the most prosperous excepting that of Jehosaphat since the time of Solomon. It is reported in the books of the Chronicles that this king did that which was pleasing in the sight of God. The death of Uzziah was therefore naturally a painful one for the prophet Isaiah. When this great king Uzziah died, Isaiah learned to move on in life and with his divine purpose.

In the year that king Uzziah died I saw also the Lord sitting upon a throne, high and lifted up, and his train filled the temple. Above it stood the seraphims: each one had six wings; with twain he covered his face, and with twain he covered his feet, and with twain he did fly. And one cried unto another, and said, Holy, holy, holy, [is]the LORD of hosts: the whole earth [is] full of his glory. And the posts of the door moved at the voice of him that cried, and the house was filled with smoke.

ISAIAH 6:1-4

Although Isaiah had lost a great king and was in such a bad circumstance, he learned to move on in life. Isaiah moved into higher dimensions in his prophetic office after the great king died. The eye of Isaiah was open to behold the beauty and the immense glory of the throne of God. In the season of an unfortunate occurrence, his eyes were opened to things he had never seen before.

In any bad circumstance and painful separation, God has under His sleeves, something great to reveal to you. There are things God will only reveal them to you in time of painful separation. The time of painful separation is the season of higher elevation in the purpose of one who finds himself in that inconvenient situation.

THE NEW MOVE OF GOD

God had been using Moses mightily in the land of Israel. When he died, the old move God began to do through Moses in the life of the children of Israel had to make way for the new move. There was going to be a new move of God through the life of Joshua. After Moses died, the children of Israel had to let go of the past and embrace the new thing God was getting ready to do.

Remember ye not the former things, neither consider the things

of old. Behold, I will do a new thing; now it shall spring forth; shall ye not know it? I will even make a way in the wilderness, [and] rivers in the desert.

ISAIAH 43:18-19

When we hold on so much to the past, God cannot do anything new in our lives. There is no need to complain about how things are not as it used to be sometime back. You do not have to waste your time looking back at the good old days. Thank God for the good old days! Your best days, however, are not behind but ahead of you.

It is interesting to notice that in the time of Moses, he had to stretch his rod for the Israelites to cross the sea and escape from the hands of the Egyptians. The waters of the sea parted when Moses stretched his rod according to the commandment of God. The children of Israel saw the deliverance of God through the stretching of the rod of Moses.

And Moses stretched out his hand over the sea; and the LORD caused the sea to go [back] by a strong east wind all that night, and made the sea dry [land,] and the waters were divided. And the children of Israel went into the midst of the sea upon the dry [ground:] and the waters [were] a wall unto them on their right hand, and on their left.

EXODUS 14:21-22

The children of Israel really saw great miracles through the stretching of a rod by Moses. When Moses died, Joshua became the leader and was supposed to lead the Israelites to cross the Jordan River. God did not resurrect Moses to stretch his rod. God used the man of the moment to give a new way of parting the waters.

Joshua was commanded by God to instruct the priest to bear the ark and step into the waters of the Jordan. When the priests obeyed the command of the new instruction of crossing the Jordan, they saw great wonders from God. The waters parted and the soles of their feet were lifted unto dry land. They did not see the miracle through the rod of Moses but their own feet stepping into the waters.

And the LORD spake unto Joshua, saying, Command the priests that bear the ark of the testimony, that they come up out of Jordan. Joshua, therefore, commanded the priests, saying, Come ye up out of Jordan. And it came to pass, when the priests that bare the ark of the covenant of the LORD were come up out of the midst of Jordan, [and] the soles of the priests' feet were lifted up unto the dry land, that the waters of Jordan returned unto their place, and flowed over all his banks, as [they did] before......On that day the LORD magnified Joshua in the sight of all Israel; and they feared him, as they feared Moses, all the days of his life.

JOSHUA 4:15-18, 14

In a difficult circumstance and a painful situation, we can easily be tempted to look back at the good old days. When we look back in the past for comfort and consolation, we will miss all that God wants for us in the "now." The greatest enemy to the new move of God is yesterday's anointing and the victories of our past. Do not hold on to past glories. Release yourself from the past and allow the new things God has for this season of your life.

CHAPTER TWO

THE SECRET OF SERVICE

THE SERVICE OF JOSHUA

And the LORD spake unto Moses face to face, as a man speaketh unto his friend. And he turned again into the camp: but his servant Joshua, the son of Nun, a young man, departed not out of the tabernacle.

EXODUS 33:11

Joshua was the servant of Moses. He served Moses in various capacities. Joshua made sure he served well. Whiles many were murmuring and speaking against Moses in difficult times, Joshua learned to stand by the great leader all the time. Whether in time of war or peace, Joshua served Moses with all his heart. Moses was sending Joshua to war in difficult and dangerous times.

Then came Amalek, and fought with Israel in Rephidim. And Moses said unto Joshua, Choose us out men, and go out, fight with Amalek: to morrow I will stand on the top of the hill with the rod of God in mine hand. So Joshua did as Moses had said to him, and fought with Amalek: and Moses, Aaron, and Hur went up to the top of the hill.

EXODUS 17:8-10

Joshua journeyed with Moses many times including a trip to receive the divine transcript from God. He became a symbol of the best example of a servant in the land of Israel. Joshua was able to tap into the secret behind service and rose up to lead the children of Israel after the death of Moses.

WHY PEOPLE FAIL TO SERVE

Many people do not want to serve. They rather want to be served than to serve others. Many leaders do not have a mind to serve but use their influence to always get their way. There are many reasons why people do not want to serve in life. If you are able to break these barriers which prevent people from serving, you will serve your way through greatness.

PRIDE

For all that [is] in the world, the lust of the flesh, and the lust of the eyes, and the pride of life, is not of the Father, but is of the world.

1 JOHN 2:16

People filled with pride are always hunting after honors, titles, and acclamation. The mouth of a proud person is a field with boasting of ancestry, family connections, great offices, honorable acquaintance, and the like. This kind of attitude does not encourage one to place himself in the position of service.

Proud people have a mind to be served rather than to serve others. They desire the praise and service of others to make them feel important and feed their pride. A person with an attitude of pride thinks serving another makes him lesser than the person he is serving. Proud people think they demean themselves when they serve others.

There is a sense of high importance in the mentality of proud people. This is a mentality which has become a hindrance in preventing people from serving. Proud people never accomplish the purpose of God for their lives. This is because every divine assignment in life requires one to be a true servant.

LACK OF THE WISDOM OF STARTING SMALL

Though thy beginning was small, yet thy latter end should greatly increase.

JOB 8:7

There is a level of service which is quite a humbling thing to do. Many do not have the wisdom of starting from a humble beginning. There is great wisdom in starting small in life. Big things done by God normally begin very small. The beginning of the great things in life starts very small.

Do not be surprised if you have to begin your divine purpose in a very humble way. The kind of service you have to offer can make people look down on you. It can even make you lose your own self-worth. The Devil will speak demeaning words in your mind when you start your divine purpose in a small way.

Do not listen to the words of the Enemy when you start small in life. The divine purpose of many of the children of God comes to an abrupt end because it is despised when it looked so small and insignificant in the beginning. They allowed the tongue of others to kill what God has begun with their lives.

LOW SELF-ESTEEM

People who have low self-esteem tend to crave to appear great in the sight of men. These people are very insecure in life and need to cover up this weakness with a desire to be served rather than to serve others. The mentality of low self-esteem fights an individual in becoming a servant.

God called many people who had a low self-esteem in the Bible. Lack of confidence had to be dealt with before they could step into their divine purpose. Low self-esteem does not make it possible for people to commit themselves to service. To them, service is just like adding salt to their wounds. They are so hungry for recognition and significance that they forget about the responsibilities which come with the privileges.

There is a search for recognition more than service with many. People who have a low self-esteem are covering up their weakness by clamoring and placing lots of titles before their names. There is nothing wrong with titles, but everything is wrong with paying attention to your titles more than the responsibilities that go with those accolades. People with low self-esteem even go to the extent of inventing titles to feed their weakness.

Many workers in the church are nowhere near the purpose of God for their lives. They are doing what they are doing because of recognition and popularity. One of the dangerous people in the world today is self-proclaimed men of God who are only searching for recognition and fame in life. Some leaders are not servants, but rather want to be served, adored, praised and become sacrosanct in the church.

WRONG PERCEPTION OF GREATNESS

There are some who search for power in order to inflict harm on people they see as enemies. Others also search for power and riches to prove a point to a father who never took care of them. Jesus noticed people in His days were living up to the expectation of others, trying to prove a point to somebody and living according to the image of greatness in the sight of men. How people loved the approval and praises of men have not changed in our time.

People love the praises of men in our time. Many are carried away by the applause of men. The world has its own definition of what greatness is. Greatness in the sight of men is wealth, power, and great influence. The image of greatness in the sight of men encourages people to be wealth-conscious and seek for power and influence by any means.

Greatness in the sight of men, however, is not the same as prominence in the sight of God. The value system of men is not the same as that of God. The image of greatness in the sight of men is not the same from the true viewpoint of God. Jesus made the assertion that greatness in the sight of men is an abomination in the sight of God. What men do not respect and look down upon are the things which are of great price in the sight of God.

And there was also a strife among them, which of them should be accounted the greatest.

LUKE 22:24

To the disciples at a point, greatness in life was to sit on a high throne and to be served by others. This perception has not changed in our world today. The wrong perception of greatness is massively creeping today among the children of God. People are fighting their way to acquire positions and titles in the church. People are paying money for positions and recognition in the church to the detriment of divine purpose.

THE MIND OF CHRIST

Let this mind be in you, which was also in Christ Jesus: Who, being in the form of God, thought it not robbery to be equal with God: But made himself of no reputation, and took upon him the form of a servant, and was made in the likeness of men:

PHILIPPIANS 2:5-7

Jesus was walking in this world with the mind of a servant. Serving and meeting the needs of people was His priority in life. When you step on the road of divine purpose, you automatically become a servant and a "victim" of divine responsibility. Your divine purpose will lead you from one level of service to another level of service all the days of your life.

It is unfortunate to realize that many who call themselves Christians do not have the mind of Christ. People who are supposed to be like Jesus are doing things differently to what He represents and came to do on this earth. Many are leading lives contrary to what Jesus represents because they are not carrying the mind of Christ.

People who call themselves Christians are chasing what Jesus was running away from in His lifetime and shunning away from what He embraced. Jesus represents a man who was not after fame, neither was He after material things in this life. Jesus is a symbol of a servant and one who was concerned about fulfilling His divine purpose.

And there was also a strife among them, which of them should be accounted the greatest. And he said unto them, The kings of the Gentiles exercise lordship over them; and they that exercise

authority upon them are called benefactors. But ye [shall] not [be] so: but he that is greatest among you, let him be as the younger; and he that is chief, as he that doth serve. For whether [is] greater, he that sitteth at meat, or he that serveth? [is] not he that sitteth at meat? but I am among you as he that serveth.

LUKE 22:24-27

The secret of service is very profound. In the kingdom of God, it is individuals serving well who are great. Significance and honor abound to one who knows the secret of service. It is this secret through which Joshua took the mantle of Moses to lead the people of God to conquer the land which had been promised.

It is this same service through which Jesus became significant in the eyes of eternity. Jesus became significant in His works on earth not by becoming the boss of all; rather the servant of all. We as Christians can never be significant in this life without the mind of Christ to serve this generation and affect generations yet unborn.

And being found in fashion as a man, he humbled himself, and became obedient unto death, even the death of the cross. Wherefore God also hath highly exalted him, and given him a name which is above every name: That at the name of Jesus every knee should bow, of [things] in heaven, and[things] in earth, and [things] under the earth; And[that] every tongue should confess that Jesus Christ [is]Lord, to the glory of God the Father.

PHILIPPIANS 2:8-11

CHAPTER THREE

THE BOOK OF PURPOSE

THE MANUAL OF PURPOSE

God revealed to Joshua a manual for his divine assignment. There is no substitute for this manual. This manual is the word of God. This is the manual you will need all your life on the journey of divine purpose. The manual is a necessary requirement to accomplish your divine assignment.

This book of the law shall not depart out of thy mouth . . . .

JOSHUA 1:8

The word of God is mighty in power. God by his word conveys strength to the weak, wisdom to the simple, comfort to the sorrowful, light to the blind, and life to the dead. The power in the manual of purpose has the capability to bring souls out of the captivity of sin into the blessed liberty of faith in Christ.

This manual of purpose is so powerful that it enters even to the deepest and most inward and secret parts of the heart, fatally wounding the stubborn, and openly reviving the believers. The word of God truly exerts so much power that any other force cannot circumvent the potency of the authority possessed by the manual.

For the word of God [is] quick, and powerful, and sharper than any two edged sword, piercing even to the dividing asunder of soul and spirit, and of the joints and marrow, and [is] a discerner of the thoughts and intents of the heart.

HEBREWS 4:12

The word of God is truly a living power. The manual of purpose is not only living but energetically efficacious. It has the potency to awaken the conscience of men. It has the ability to lay bare the secret feelings of the heart and can cause the sinner to tremble with the apprehension of the coming judgment.

All the great changes in the moral world for the better have been caused by the power of this great manual. The word of God was the foundation on which everything exists. Also, everything exists because of purpose. The power in this great manual called the word of God was able to form the material fabric of the universe.

Through faith we understand that the worlds were framed by the word of God, so that things which are seen were not made of things which do appear.

HEBREWS 11:3

The matter itself of which heaven and earth are made was called into existence by God's power in His word. This same word was that which brought the world into order and beauty. We need supernatural power to carry us through the purpose of God for our lives. Without exercising the power in the manual, we are doomed to be failures in the eyes of eternity.

It does not matter the amount of wealth, honor, and power you may possess in life, you need the manual more than any other thing. Living life without the manual can produce vain honor and polluted wealth. Your achievement in this life is nothing without the manual which guides you into the purpose of God for your life. You will lose your own soul if you fail to allow the manual of the word of God to guard your heart and guide your steps.

The word of God will navigate your steps in life for you to go all the lengths of your assignment in life. It is a terrible thing to reject the manual for your purpose in life. Your God-given destiny will be lost in the sea of eternity if you fail to take heed and apply the word of God.

THE TREASURE OF THE WORD OF GOD

God has a purpose for each one of us. In order for us to operate in our calling, we need the word of God to guide us. Many children of God have been rendered inactive as far as their purpose in life is concerned. This is because many of them do not have quality time in studying the word of God.

Many of the wealthy millionaires and billionaires we know of are not *born again* and yet are very rich and are perceived as successful. It is, therefore, possible to be great in the sight of men but failures in the eyes of God. Many have abundance in goods but bankrupt of the word of God and the effectiveness of accomplishing the divine purpose.

Because thou sayest, I am rich, and increased with goods, and have need of nothing; and knowest not that thou art wretched, and miserable, and poor, and blind, and naked:

REVELATION 3:17

The way men perceive us may be entirely the opposite to what is real in the eyes of eternity. There are many, who are heirs of the kingdom of this world but abject slaves in the sight of God. Many of the children of God are also bringing great results in all facets of life and yet poverty is found at the doorsteps of their purpose in life.

The manual to bring out the efficiency in our purpose has been relegated to the background. I do not believe in reading the Bible for five minutes we call Quiet Time in the morning and be efficient in our calling. The Bible should not just be read for few minutes as a ritual but it must be studied and its words meditated.

You studied your lecture notes and did vigorous research and yet failed that very exam you wrote. How do you think by reading the Bible casually will bring anything substantial. Are we not joking as children of God? Are we not deceiving ourselves BIG TIME? The fact is that we read more on social media than our Bibles. Christians of today have availed ourselves more to television than the manual which will help us in fulfill the reason why we appeared on the earth.

Study to shew thyself approved unto God, a workman that needeth not to be ashamed, rightly dividing the word of truth.

2 TIMOTHY 2:15

It is shameful for a Christian to have an Oxford Dictionary but not a Bible Dictionary. Many Christians lack research tools for studying the word of God. Your efficiency in life is dependent upon the tools you have. By just looking at the tools you have in your possession, I can tell the kind of furnished products you are going to produce. A gifted carpenter cannot do much with 17th century carpentry tools.

THE POWER OF MEDITATION

Only be thou strong and very courageous, that thou mayest observe to do according to all the law, which Moses my servant commanded thee: turn not from it [to] the right hand or [to] the left, that thou mayest prosper whithersoever thou goest. This book of the law shall not depart out of thy mouth; but thou

shalt MEDITATE THEREIN DAY AND NIGHT, that thou mayest observe to do according to all that is written therein: for then thou shalt make thy way prosperous, and then thou shalt have good success.

JOSHUA 1:7-8

This divine instruction was given by God to Joshua who was mandated to take the children of Israel into the Promised Land. In executing this particular purpose for his life, the key for success in his calling was the power of meditation. You must understand that Joshua was a General of the Army of Israel who was supposed to use the sword and the spear to conquer the inhabitants of the Promised Land.

God did not instruct Joshua to learn more skills in handling the sword and throwing of the spear. His ability to fulfill the purpose of God for his life was not dependent upon the use of the sword but was in the power of meditation. According to the divine instruction to Joshua, meditation of the word of God was the key to making his way prosperous.

The word *prosperous* in scripture does not mean driving expensive cars or building mansions. We should not make the error to interpret every scripture to temporal riches and material things. *Prosperity* here simply means executing his divine purpose successfully. Men measure prosperity by material gains but wealth in the eyes of Heaven is your effectiveness in accomplishing the purpose of God for your life.

Meditation of the word of God is able to bring true prosperity. He who is ready to prosper in the calling of God for his life must delight in meditating the word of God and not to withdraw his mind from it. No spiritual exercise is more profitable to the soul than that of devout meditation. As the miser often returns to look upon his treasure, so does the devout believer by frequent meditation turn to the priceless wealth which he has discovered in the book of the Lord.

The manual for every purpose is certainly the word of God! The word of God needs to be activated for us to tap into its power and potency. The fullness of the power of God can be harnessed through meditation. The power of meditation can release the potency of the word of God to navigate our paths in the journey to our divine destination.

Meditation of the word of God is to ponder on the words of life. The word of life is able to guide every footstep you make in this life. Effective meditation always involves self-examination and reflection. Although prayer is a powerful tool of the believer, it is not a substitute of self-examination and reflection.

This is the reason why it is possible to return from a forty day fast and still have the same wrong perceptions in life. As much as we need more prayer in the Body of Christ, we equally need self-examination and reflection. Divine strength and courage of the Almighty are tapped for our divine purpose when we learn to meditate upon the word of God.

Only be thou strong and very courageous, that thou mayest observe to do according to all the law, which Moses my servant commanded thee: turn not from it [to] the right hand or [to] the left, that thou mayest prosper whithersoever thou goest. This book of the law shall not depart out of thy mouth; but thou shalt MEDITATE THEREIN DAY AND NIGHT, that thou mayest observe to do according to all that is written therein: for then thou shalt make thy way prosperous, and then thou shalt have good success.

JOSHUA 1:7-8

This was an important divine instruction to Joshua who was mandated to take the children of Israel into the Promised Land. His ability to fulfill the purpose of God for his life was not dependent upon the use of the sword but was in the power of meditation. According to the divine instruction to Joshua, meditation of the word of God was the key in making his way prosperous. In executing this particular purpose for his life, the key for success in Joshua's calling was through the power of meditation.

CHAPTER FOUR

SIX DIMENSIONS OF THE COURAGE OF JOSHUA

THE MENTAL STRENGTH TO VENTURE INTO NEW TERRITORIES

On the road of purpose, God will lead us to many new territories. It takes a lot of courage to venture into new areas in life. It takes much to do uncommon things. People who do uncommon things in this life are criticized and misrepresented. Your purpose in this life is unique, so you will need a lot of courage to launch into new areas of life.

The land which God promised the children of Israel was a new territory for them. It was a land they had never seen before and a place they have never ventured before. God always has a new place for your feet to tread. God wants to do something new in your life and you need the mental strength to venture into your Promised Land.

At a point in time, Moses could discern in his spirit that God had started doing something new in the life of his servant Joshua. Through Joshua, God was going to take His people into the Promised Land. Moses, therefore, knew that Joshua was going to need mental courage to venture into this new territory.

And he gave Joshua the son of Nun a charge, and said, Be strong and of a good courage: for thou shalt bring the children of Israel into the land which I sware unto them: and I will be with thee.

DEUTERONOMY 31:23

For Joshua to lead the children of Israel into the Promised Land, he needed a lot of courage. There is a Promised Land in the life of every child of God. This land is an uncommon endeavor among humanity. For you to enter into your land, you need a lot of mental courage. You need to be strong in the mind to venture into new areas in life.

Be strong and of a good courage: for unto this people shalt thou divide for an inheritance the land, which I sware unto their fathers to give them.

JOSHUA 1:6

You must have the power of imagination to nurse the vision God has placed in your heart. As you nurse the vision in your heart through prayer and confession of the word of God, you begin to deposit mental courage in your life in order to venture into new areas and dimensions in life.

THE MENTAL STRENGTH TO PERSEVERE

And he spake a parable unto them [to this end,]that men ought always to pray, and not to faint; Saying, There was in a city a judge, which feared not God, neither regarded man: And there was a widow in that city; and she came unto him, saying, Avenge me of mine adversary. And he would not for a while: but afterward, he said within himself, Though I fear not God, nor regard man; Yet because this widow troubleth me, I will avenge her, lest by her continual coming she weary me.

LUKE 18:1-5

This was a wonderful parable told by Jesus. The parable is designed to teach us that, though our prayers should long appear to be unanswered, we should persevere, and not grow weary in supplication to God. We can learn something about perseverance from the widow in this parable.

Perseverance is very important in getting all the things God has for you. Without perseverance, we will give up easily with the things God wants us to have and the dimensions He desires us to enter. Many people give up easily in life and never become what God wants them to become in this life.

Joshua could never have become what God wanted him to become without the strength of showing courage by perseverance. God told Joshua never to give up in this life no matter what happens. Many easily give up in life and never become what God wants them to become.

Have not I commanded thee? Be strong and of a good courage; be not afraid, neither be thou dismayed: for the LORD thy God is with thee whithersoever thou goest.

JOSHUA 1:9

Joshua was not supposed to throw his hands in the air with despair on the road of his divine purpose for any reason. He was to accomplish his purpose in life with much perseverance. With much perseverance brings better results in every facet of life. Do not give up on the vision God has placed in your heart. Rise up every time you fall to fight and give it another try.

MENTAL STRENGTH TO SHOW URGENCY

Moses sent twelve leaders in Israel to spy the land God had promised. These were noble and great men in the land of Israel. Among the twelve spies, ten came with a bad report concerning the Promised Land. They brought a report on the strength and fearsomeness of the inhabitants of the land.

And they brought up an evil report of the land which they had searched unto the children of Israel, saying, The land, through which we have gone to search it, is a land that eateth up the inhabitants thereof; and all the people that we saw in it [are] men of a great stature. And there we saw the giants, the sons of

Anak, [which come] of the giants: and we were in our own sight as grasshoppers, and so we were in their sight.

NUMBERS 13:32-33

Joshua and Caleb had a different spirit from those ten who brought the evil report. These two were not only sure of victory over the inhabitants of the land but showed urgency in conquering the Promised Land. These two men showed urgency concerning the promise of God to the nation of Israel.

And Caleb stilled the people before Moses, and said, let us go up at once, and possess it; for we are well able to overcome it.

NUMBERS 13:30

Some people know what to do but do not show any urgency. Showing of urgency comes from the mind. It is not just enough to believe in the promises of God and be hesitant in pursuing. It is important for us to show urgency in all that we do. We may know the purpose of God for our lives, but we need the mental strength of urgency to accomplish.

Showing urgency is not a sign of impatience. It is having the knowledge of the will of God and going straight at it without procrastination and giving of excuses. It is to know that we must work the works of Him that sent us whiles it is day. No man can work when we enter the dark period of our lives.

MENTAL STRENGTH TO "DISCARD" UNWANTED PEOPLE

God told Joshua to "discard" and part ways with all those who will not hearken unto his words. It does not matter how nice the person is, he must do away with all those who fall short of the standards of God. Joshua needed a lot of guts to part ways with those who did not believe in his divine destiny.

Whosoever he be that doth rebel against thy commandment, and will not hearken unto thy words in all that thou commandest him, he shall be put to death: only be strong and of a good courage.

JOSHUA 1:18

We are here admonished to kill any relationship which does not fuel us in accomplishing the purpose of God. On the road of divine purpose, we need to cultivate in our minds the mental strength to cut off unwanted people in our lives. There are many people around you who have no part to play in your life.

Some people want to embrace everybody that comes into their lives. There are many people in our lives who are not relevant as far as the purpose of God for our lives is concerned. These are excess baggage we try carrying on the journey of purpose. These people we carry along do not have any relation nor has bearing with the vision God placed in our hearts.

MENTAL STRENGTH TO SEIZE

God has placed so many things on the path of your divine purpose. You need a lot of mental strength to be able to seize the things God has placed in your way. The land that God gave to the children of Israel was already inhabited. In fact, God did not promise them a land which was empty of people.

Moses heard from God that the land they were to possess was already occupied by the Gentiles. There were many tribes living on the Promised Land. God did not give them a land which was vacant but one that already had inhabitants. The inhabitants were not weak people, but were very strong and giants in the land.

And they told him, and said, We came unto the land whither thou sentest us, and surely it floweth with milk and honey; and this [is] the fruit of it. Nevertheless the people [be] strong

that dwell in the land, and the cities [are] walled, [and] very great: and moreover we saw the children of Anak there. The Amalekites dwell in the land of the south: and the Hittites, and the Jebusites, and the Amorites, dwell in the mountains: and the Canaanites dwell by the sea, and by the coast of Jordan.

NUMBERS 13:27-29

Joshua needed to seize the Promised Land from the inhabitants of the land. He needed mental strength to seize what God had already promised. Moses foresaw how Joshua needed so much courage in order to possess the land. He, therefore, gave a charge to Joshua to be strong in order to seize the land.

And Moses called unto Joshua, and said unto him in the sight of all Israel, Be strong and of a good courage: for thou must go with this people unto the land which the LORD hath sworn unto their fathers to give them; and thou shalt cause them to inherit it.

DEUTERONOMY 31:7

MENTAL STRENGTH TO RETAIN

It was the plan of God not only for the children of Israel to seize the Promised Land. It was also in the plan of God for them to retain the land by possessing it. God does not only want you to seize the things He has placed on your path, He expects you to possess and not to lose it.

Many people are able to seize things God has placed on their path, but few are able to keep them and not lose them. The mental strength to retain and posses is as important as the capacity to seize what God has placed on your path. Joshua was not only commanded to seize the land but also to possess it and not to lose it.

Then ye shall drive out all the inhabitants of the land from before you, and destroy all their pictures, and destroy all their molten images, and quite pluck down all their high places: And

ye shall dispossess [the inhabitants] of the land, **and dwell therein: for i have given you the land to possess it.**

NUMBERS 33:52-53

Allowing what God has placed in your hands to slip away is a very unfortunate incidence. This, however, occurs in the life of many of the children of God. For you to be significant in the eyes of God, you need to have the mental strength not only to seize but to possess as well. This was exactly what Joshua did and became significant in the eyes of God.

And I said unto you, Ye are come unto the mountain of the Amorites, which the LORD our God doth give unto us. Behold, the LORD thy God hath set the land before thee: go up [and] possess [it,] as the LORD God of thy fathers hath said unto thee; fear not, neither be discouraged.

DEUTERONOMY 1:20-21

CHAPTER FIVE

CONTENDING FOR THE PROMISE

THE PROMISE TO ISRAEL

God promised the children of Israel of a great land they were to inherit. This was promised when they were slaves in the land of Egypt and going through so many afflictions. God promised them of a prosperous land and one flowing with milk and honey. God appeared to Moses and spoke to him about the Promised Land.

And the LORD said, I have surely seen the affliction of my people which [are] in Egypt, and have heard their cry by reason of their taskmasters; for I know their sorrows; And I am come down to deliver them out of the hand of the Egyptians, and to bring them up out of that land unto a good land and a large, unto a land flowing with milk and honey; unto the place of the Canaanites, and the Hittites, and the Amorites, and the Perizzites, and the Hivites, and the Jebusites.

EXODUS 3:7-8

Moses heard in his ears wonderful prophesies concerning the children of Israel. This was very soothing and exciting prophesies for the children of Israel. They had been in bondage for many decades in Egypt and finally heard a very exciting prophesy about their emancipation and prosperity.

There is an unfortunate story behind this story. Among those who came from the land of Egypt, only Joshua and Caleb were able to enter the Promised Land. All the rest of the people who heard this prophesy were not able to enter into the land flowing with milk and honey. Many went out of the land of Egypt but only two among the masses were able to receive the promise of God.

While it is said, Today if ye will hear his voice, harden not your hearts, as in the provocation. For some, when they had heard, did provoke: howbeit not all that came out of Egypt by Moses. But with whom was he grieved forty years? [was it]not with them that had sinned, whose carcases fell in the wilderness? And to whom sware he that they should not enter into his rest, but to them that believed not? So we see that they could not enter in because of unbelief.

HEBREWS 3:15-19

THE MYSTERY OF PROPHECY

The Bible is a book of prophecies. Prophesy is about foretelling of future events, by inspiration from God. Prophesy is very different from just a calculated conjecture of events in the future. True prophecy is also not from a vague and equivocal oracle, without any certain meaning. A true and pure prophecy can come only from God.

A true prophecy may be known by some characteristics. Prophesy must be announced at a suitable time before the event it foretells, having an exact agreement with a specific event. Another important characteristic of prophecy is the right instrument of the declaration. True prophecy must be delivered by one who is under the inspiration of the Almighty.

Many of the prophecies of scripture foretold events ages before they occurred. Events of which there was then no apparent probability, and the occurrence of which depended on innumerable contingencies, involving the history of things and the volitions of persons not then in existence; and yet these predictions were fulfilled at the time and place and in the manner prophesied.

However, it is important to understand that there are levels of the prophetic. There is a level of prophecy which no flesh nor can spirit abort. An example of this level of the prophetic is the coming of the Messiah. Another important prophecy at this level is the end of this age. This level of the prophetic cannot be interrupted by any entity in heaven, on the earth nor under the sea because it has been sealed.

THE CONDITIONAL PROPHESY

There is also another level of the prophetic which cannot be categorized on the same level to the coming of the Messiah nor the end of the age. This level of the prophetic does not happen by default. With this level of the prophetic, a particular prophecy can fail when vital parties fail to play their roles.

And it shall come to pass, IF thou shalt hearken diligently unto the voice of the LORD thy God, to observe [and] to do all his commandments which I command thee this day, that the LORD thy God will set thee on high above all nations of the earth: And all these blessings shall come on thee, and overtake thee, IF thou shalt hearken unto the voice of the LORD thy God.

DEUTERONOMY 28:1-2

This is an example of prophecy which will only see the day of light by a specific condition being met. The prophecy came to the children of Israel through Moses in the wilderness. This prophecy was only going to come to pass if they obeyed the commandments of God. The children of Israel were going to be exalted above all nations only on condition that they hearken unto the word of God and obey. Their national obedience was to be rewarded by extraordinary and universal prosperity according to the prophecy.

It was only those who run in the way of God's conditions concerning the prophecies that were going to experience the abundance of blessings. Those who positioned themselves by their behavior and attitude contrary to the condition of the prophecy were going to reap the reversal penalty of the promise.

But it shall come to pass, if thou wilt not hearken unto the voice of the LORD thy God, to observe to do all his commandments and his statutes which I command thee this day; that all these curses shall come upon thee, and overtake thee: Cursed [shalt] thou [be] in the city, and cursed [shalt] thou [be] in the field. Cursed[shall be] thy basket and thy store. Cursed [shall be] the fruit of thy body, and the fruit of thy land, the increase of thy kine, and the flocks of thy sheep. Cursed [shalt] thou [be] when thou comest in, and cursed [shalt] thou [be] when thou goest out. The LORD shall send upon thee cursing, vexation, and rebuke, in all that

thou settest thine hand unto for to do, until thou be destroyed, and until thou perish quickly; because of the wickedness of thy doings, whereby thou hast forsaken me.

DEUTERONOMY 28:15-20

Prophesy from God can turn into curses when we fail to meet the conditions concerning that particular prophecy. Many people are excited when a prophecy comes concerning how God wants to bless them and many run to the places where they are likely to receive prophesies. As much as God wants to bless you, Satan also desires for you to walk in curses.

There is nothing wrong with hearing prophecies about how God wants to bless us. You must understand however that, this kind of prophecy cannot match up to the same level as the prophecy of the second coming of the Messiah. The level of prophecy concerning the many great things God will do in your life is most of the time not automatic. It is true that God has great plans for your life but you must understand that this level of prophecy may be conditional.

Your failure to meet this same condition of prophecies concerning the blessings of God will turn into great curses. The prophecy you heard concerning how God wants to bestow His blessings on you only reveals the original intention of God for your life. It reveals the conception of your purpose in the mind of God.

The prophecy concerning how God wants to exalt you and bestow His blessings upon your life is likely conditional. This level of prophecy only navigates into the womb of the mind of God to reveal what has been captured about your purpose. That which has been conceived in the womb is not an automatic candidate for life. It is your responsibility to nourish what is conceived and PUSH the purpose from the womb into reality.

CONTENDING FOR YOUR PROPHESY THROUGH PRAYER

There is no doubt about the magnificence of the purpose of God concerning your life. The Almighty only conceives great things in His mind. The conception of your purpose in the mind of God exceeds the imagination of men. You have a part to play to transport this great purpose from the mind of God into reality.

You are expected to contend for the prophecy concerning your life. Your purpose in this life is a prophecy which must be contended at all cost before it can be manifested in your life. The proclamation of your prophecy is to put you on the alert to transport your purpose from eternity to time through the power of prayer.

Prophesy also comes to show you your end in times of difficulties and hopelessness to inspire you to push and forge ahead rather than giving up on your divine destiny. When you fail to push your prayer from the womb in times of difficulties, your "baby" will never see the light of day. Prophesy comes to give you the assurance of your end so that you will be encouraged to push more for the prophecy to come to pass.

As an ultrasound scan reveals the identity and gender of a baby to inspire a mother to push on the day of delivery, so does the word of prophecy comes to show you what to expect when you do not give up on what has been promised. When prophecy is proclaimed about your life, you must pray and fast as never before. This is because the word of prophecy has come to expose that which had been conceived in the mind of God and now open to the attacks of Satan.

Many people go to sleep after receiving prophecy with joy of the great things God is going to do in their lives. Prophecy is dangerous when you go to sleep! The proclamation of prophecy will result in more attempted attacks in your life as never before. Proclamation of prophecy is supposed to put us on the red alert to pray and push what has been conceived in the mind of God into existence.

POWER TO PUSH

When a woman is pregnant with a child, a day comes where she has to travail and push the baby out. The baby will continue to remain in the womb as long as the woman refuses to push to force the baby out. Prayer is the power to push our purpose into fruition. Through prayer, our purpose is transported from eternity in the mind of God to time.

Who hath heard such a thing? who hath seen such things? Shall the earth be made to bring forth in one day? [or] shall a nation be born at once? for as soon as Zion travailed, she brought forth her children.

ISAIAH 66:8

Your purpose is like a baby in the womb of a woman. The manifestation of your purpose does not happen instantly. Your purpose must first be conceived in the womb of the mind of God. It takes time and process for the earth to bring forth plants. Your purpose in life must also go through a process before its manifestation.

Rome they say was not built in a day. Your purpose in life will also not be manifested in a twinkle of an eye. Your purpose is like building a city which takes hard work and great sacrifice. Without hard work and sacrifice, your purpose will ever remain in the mind of God and never to be manifested among men. A woman never brings forth a child without hard work and sacrifice.

It is a natural order for a pregnant woman to travail before she hears the cry of her baby. The woman is responsible for pushing her own miracle which is the baby. Nobody can pray for you to push your purpose from eternity to time. You are responsible for the manifestation of your purpose in life. You need to indulge yourself in consistent and habitual prayers to push your purpose to manifestation.

And it came to pass in the time of her travail, that, behold, twins [were] in her womb.

GENESIS 38:27

This part of the scripture was the travail of Tamar who was pregnant by her own father in-law; Judah. Tamar never knew she was carrying twins till she pushed at the time of her travail. She never knew what was in her womb till she decided to push. You will never come to a full realization of the magnanimity of your purpose when you fail to pray to push your purpose.

For since the beginning of the world [men] have not heard, nor perceived by the ear, neither hath the eye seen, O God, beside thee, [what] he hath prepared for him that waiteth for him.

ISAIAH 64:4

The entire world has been strangers to your purpose in life all along. God's glory concerning your purpose has never been seen or heard of. No man has perceived and understood the value and beauty of those things which God has prepared for his people concerning their purpose.

Your purpose has never entered into the mind of a man nor could any intelligence decipher but that of God. Only the mind of God can conceive such a big plan and so vast a project. It is only God's power through prayer that can push your purpose from eternity to time, for it to be manifested among men. Prayer will bring your purpose into full effect.

God's purpose is manifested in the lives of people who tarry in prayer to push their miracle out of the womb. Even after taping into the mind of God by His Spirit concerning your purpose, you will even have to push harder because the manifestation of your purpose is at hand. When you are diligent in prayer, you will push your purpose out for the manifestation of all flesh. Joshua contended for the prophecy with the sword, but you will need the sword of the Spirit which is the word of God and the power of prayer to enter into your prophetic destiny.

THE END

9 789988 886745

footsteps of Joshua in the Bible. It is an in-depth magnifier to discover the principles used by Joshua to write his name with gold in this life and the life that is to come. As we learn from the people of old we will better understand the ways of God. The heroes of faith lived in different eras of life and came from diverse backgrounds. In an interesting era of the age of the world today, the foundation that the people of old stood on to stand tall above their enemies still works forever. Join me in this microscopic view of aspects of the life of Joshua.

Feather Brained
Winslow Swan

Feather Brained
Winslow Swan

Copyright 2014 Winslow Swan

Other Works by this author
The Convincer
Click (A Tale Of Revenge)
Toppling Over The Edge
Evil Within
Do Not Read This Book
The Suicide Killers: The First Jake Rhodes Mystery
More Stories To Read To The Thing Under The Bed
Ten Twisted Tales From The Maelstrom

License Notes
Thank you for downloading this fee ebook. Although this is a free book, it remains the copyrighted property of the author, and may not be reproduced, copied and distributed for commercial or non-commercial purposes. If you enjoyed this book, please encourage your friends to download their own copy at Amazon.com, where they can also discover other works by this author. Thank you for your support.